LIFE IN THE
– U.S. –
NATIONAL GUARD

by Mo Barrett

Published by Pebble, an imprint of Capstone
1710 Roe Crest Drive, North Mankato, Minnesota 56003
capstonepub.com

Library of Congress Cataloging-in-Publication Data is available on the Library of Congress website.

ISBN: 9780756579906 (hardcover)
ISBN: 9780756580124 (paperback)
ISBN: 9780756579968 (ebook PDF)

Summary: Gives readers a peak into daily life for U.S. National Guardsmen.

Editorial Credits
Editor: Mandy Robbins; Designer: Heidi Thompson; Media Researcher: Jo Miller;
Production Specialist: Tori Abraham

Image Credits
Alaska National Guard photo by Sgt. Seth LaCount, 15; Getty Images: monkeybusinessimages, 5,
Moyo Studio, 21; Louisiana National Guard photo by Spc. Rashawn Price, Cover (top left); Oklahoma
National Guard photo by Sgt. Anthony Jones, 19; Shutterstock: Picksell, background (throughout),
Prostock-studio, 18; U.S Air Force photo by Master Sgt. Mark Olsen, 9; U.S. Air National Guard photo
by Airman 1st Class Cody Witsaman, Cover (top right), Phil Speck, Cover (bottom), Senior Airman
John Linzmeier, 17, Staff Sgt. Anthony Agosti, 14, Tech. Sgt. Amber Monio, 11, 13, Tech. Sgt. Joshua
Allmaras, Cover (top middle); U.S. Army National Guard photo by Bill Valentine, 10, Sgt. Michael
Uribe, 7

TABLE OF CONTENTS

Words in **bold** appear in the glossary.

YOUR NEIGHBORHOOD GUARD MEMBERS

Members of the National Guard are **civilians** first. They may be your neighbor, your coach, or your parent. They train and serve in the military as a part-time job. The rest of the time, they may work other jobs and live regular lives.

WHERE NATIONAL GUARDSMEN LIVE

Members of the National Guard serve where they live. The National Guard is in all 50 states, Washington, D.C., and other U.S. **territories**. If there is an emergency in a state, its governor calls the National Guard to help.

Georgia National Guardsmen unload supplies for Georgia residents facing a winter storm.

WHAT NATIONAL GUARDSMEN DO

National Guard members must be ready for anything. They are on call to help with local emergencies. There might be a bad storm or natural disaster. Sometimes they back up local police. Or they could be sent to **combat** to back up other military branches.

National Guardsmen board a plane for Afghanistan to support Operation Enduring Freedom.

National Guard members can have any job. Some are doctors. Some are teachers. Some drive trucks. Some work with computers. A National Guard member might have skills from their civilian job that help in their military job.

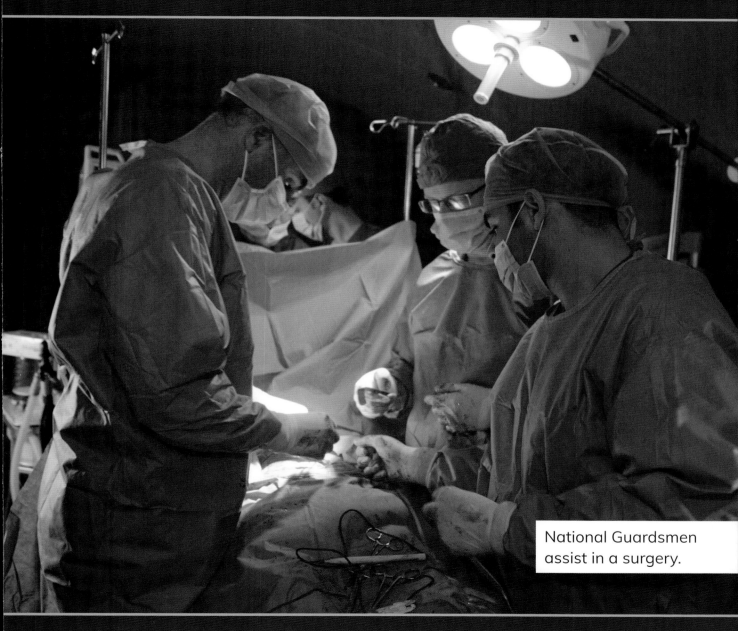

National Guardsmen assist in a surgery.

HOW NATIONAL GUARDSMEN TRAIN

Guard members go to official military training centers one weekend a month. Once a year, they go for two weeks straight. Guard members train to prepare for military duties. They learn **teamwork** and leadership. They learn to use special tools and equipment.

National Guard members must stay in shape. Once a year, they take a fitness test. They must be able to run, carry heavy things, and crawl through tight spaces.

One guardsman assists another in putting on his protective wear for a training drill.

SERVING AT HOME

A National Guard member might be at their regular job. They get a call that they are needed for local military service. They will put on their military **uniform** to help people nearby.

Guard members give out supplies after a natural disaster. They might clean up public places and make sure streets are safe to drive on. When there is a big event, they set up seating and direct traffic. They also help the police keep everyone safe.

SERVING ABROAD

When the President of the United States needs more military help, he calls on the National Guard. Your teacher might be at school today. Next month, she may be in a military uniform.

National Guard members are sent all over the world. They may leave their families for months to serve.

Guardsmen sit aboard an airplane being transported to Poland.

When members travel far from home, they also leave their regular jobs. There are rules to protect their job while they are away. When they get back, they go back to their regular job. Their military service makes these everyday heroes an important part of your local **community**.

Families celebrate guardsmen at a welcome-back ceremony.

DRAW A NATIONAL GUARDSMAN

Imagine you are in the National Guard. What job would you want to do in the National Guard? What job do you want to do in your regular job? Can you draw yourself changing from your regular clothes into your military uniform like a superhero?

GLOSSARY

civilian (suh-VIL-yuhn)—a person who is not in the military

combat (KOM-bat)—fighting between people or armies

community (kuh-MYOO-nuh-tee)—a group of people who live in the same area

teamwork (TEEM-wurk)—people working together toward the same goal

territory (TER-uh-tor-ee)—an area under the control of a country but not part of that country

uniform (YOU-nuh-form)—special clothing that members of a particular group wear

READ MORE

Gagliardi, Sue. *US National Guard*. Mendota Heights, MN: Apex Editions, 2023.

Miller, Marie-Therese. *The US National Guard in Action*. Minneapolis: Lerner Publications, 2023.

Morey, Allan. *U.S. National Guard*. Minneapolis: Pogo Books, 2021.

INTERNET SITES

The National Guard Explained
youtube.com/watch?v=c0aPTBy0MpA

United States National Guard Facts for Kids
kids.kiddle.co/United_States_National_Guard

What Is the National Guard?
youtube.com/watch?v=F3voQKDRc_Q

INDEX

ABOUT THE AUTHOR

Mo Barrett is a retired Colonel. She spent nearly 30 years in the Air Force flying as a pilot and setting up airfields. She is now a public speaker and entertainer using humor to change the way people laugh, learn and think.